Holy Cross Class of '72 Ex-Man

Gordon T. Davis

ISBN: 1-4609-1862-2
ISBN-13: 9781460918623

Preface

Holy Cross College in Worcester MA changed my life profoundly. The following are memories from that time.

Some of the stories are about people that you may have heard about such as Edward P. Jones (Pulitzer Prize winner for fiction), Ted Wells (who defended Scooter Libby), Clarence Thomas, and others. You probably have not heard of most of the others in the book, but they all played a part in history of the College and the City of Worcester. These memories are how the events shaped us and we them.

The Class of 1972 has, even today, a reputation as being the most radical class in the history of Holy Cross. Many of us never graduated and we became what is known today as Ex-men.

I want to thank everyone who helped me write these stories, especially Ed Jones.

The cover photo was taken during a rally for jobs in 2010 and appeared in the Worcester Telegram.

Chapter 1
The Trip to Heaven

The priests locked the doors to the school in the middle of day which was unusual. We were told to remain in our seats. Several hundred kids from Olney High School were marching up the street. I was a senior at Cardinal Dougherty High School in Philadelphia Pennsylvania.

It was a Friday in April 1968 and the Reverend Dr. Martin Luther King, Jr. had been murdered. Olney High School was and still is a public school in Philadelphia. No one knew what the Olney High kids intended to do. They stopped in front of Cardinal Dougherty for several minutes saying nothing I could hear and then left. They had walked out of school at the news of Dr. King's assassination. Harvey, a classmate who was a friend with some of the students from Olney, told us that they wanted us to join their march. Sometimes I wondered how different my life would have been, if I could have joined with the Olney students that day. I probably would not had been made aware of the visit by the Admission Director at Holy Cross, Mr. Gallagher. I had a bad reputation already among the administrators and walking out to join the Olney kids would have been another negative.

A week after Dr. King had been killed, Harvey and I were called into the Guidance Office. Jim Gallagher, Director of Admissions at College of the Holy Cross, offered us a chance to compete for an academic scholarship. He described the College as all male mostly Irish Catholic and located 300 miles north and 40 miles from Boston in a mill town, Worcester, Massachusetts.

In 1968 and still today a scholarship has been a once in a lifetime opportunity because it simultaneously relieved my parents' financial burden and deferred me from going to war. Like many of my classmates, I faced a fast approaching compulsory draft.

The Guidance Office never explained why it selected Harvey and me as the favored scholarship recipients to Holy Cross. Cardinal Dougherty tracked its students based on homerooms. The first two homerooms had advanced courses. Harvey and I were in the third homeroom, where there were academically capable kids who somehow never fit into the advanced homerooms.

A possible reason we were chosen was that there was only one Black male student, Rodger, in the advanced home rooms and he had accepted a scholarship to St. Joseph College in Philadelphia.

At the meeting Jim Gallagher invited me to take a tour of the campus the next weekend. Harvey, Mr. Gallager and I were accompanied by Father Brooks, Ed, Perry, Walter, Craig, and one other student whose name I just cannot remember as he was not accepted at the College.

Mr. Gallagher rented a station wagon and we headed north on our seven hours trip to Worcester. I was a little confused by it all, but my parents were most happy because this trip finally answered my dad's question about whether I would join the Army, the priesthood, or go to college.

My father was a career soldier who became disenchanted with the Army. When he was discharged in 1962 he then worked as a mechanic. He warned me against the Army; he said that I would be unhappy and I would be killed in Vietnam. He also said that I would be unhappy in the priesthood. Later in life I realized that my dad knew me better than I knew myself and how much he and my mom loved me, despite my rebelliousness.

The road trip to Worcester was long; even longer for Ed who had taken a bus from Washington D. C. to meet us in Philadelphia. Mr. Gallagher spoke more than Father Brooks. Harvey and Walter spoke more than the rest of us. It is ironic that I spoke more to Father Brooks that day than I would speak with him subsequently.

Halfway through the trip a news bulletin was announced on the radio. Black students at Columbia University had taken over their administration building to protest the War and racism. Little did I know I would be engaged in the same fight for justice at Holy Cross next Fall. The song that I remembered the most during the ride was "Tighten Up" by Archie Bell and the Drells. I saw the group in 2010 on a PBS special and I could not help but think how dated they looked

It was nightfall when we finally arrived at Holy Cross. At the Junction of 195 and 191 Father Brooks almost made a wrong turn. If he had, the trip would had been two hours longer. Ed remembers that Father Brooks actually made the wrong turn. Regardless everyone was hungry when we got to campus. We first tried to find food at Kimball dining hall, but it was closed. We got some food from Hogan campus center.

Mr. Gallagher asked who had a license to drive and I said I did. He then asked me to drive the station wagon to a parking place behind Fenwick. In doing so I accidently went forward when I had intended to go in reverse. Although I did not hit anything Mr. Gallagher said we needed the station wagon to get back to Philly.

I stayed at the newer Lehy Dormitory on what would be later called Easy Street. Compared to my room in my Philadelphia home, the dorm room in Lehy was perfect. It had a dedicated closet, bureaus, mirror, and a desk. As a working-class kid, these amenities were sometimes missing. I did not have a closet or a mirror with a lamp at home in Philly. The room felt orderly and uncluttered. Holy Cross was a predominantly White campus, but that night we met half of the Black students, Ron, Tim, Art, and Bob. I was told that there were only eight Black students total attending Holy Cross in the Spring of 1968.

The next morning a maid entered my room and made the bed. She was very pleasant. I had mixed feeling about this, because my mother worked as a maid at a local college in the Philadelphia area after losing her union job in the ladies garment industry. The thought of any one making up my bed was disorienting, even more so when she was a White woman. I know now that any working class student would have experienced the same disorientation. When I worked at Holy Cross in 2005, an administrator from North Carolina said that she also experienced disorientation when White people would serve her during events.

I attended a Political Science class that Saturday. Half- way through the class I knew that Political Science was unlikely as a major. Talking with the other prospective students, it became obvious I was the only one to attend a class. They went off doing more interesting things.

For lunch we ate in Kimball Hall, which was a mesmerizing and somewhat majestic place. I took a seat at one of the long heavy wooden tables and I curiously watched as White students waiters served my food.

Afterwards I met some more students on campus then prepared for the evening concert in the athletic Field House. Ray Charles was scheduled to perform and we all were excited about the show. It was the first concert I ever attended given by professional performers whose music was on the radio. The opening act was a jazz big band and they were great. I would have been happy just listening to them. Then came Ray Charles, hearing him in person was otherworldly. My closest previous experience was listening to the parish choir singing at Midnight Mass on Christmas. I felt like I was going to heaven and I made up my mind to go to Holy Cross.

Chapter 2
Holding onto HHH

My first bus ride to Worcester in August of 1968 was seemingly unending, especially with the layover in New York City. The Worcester bus station then was on Front St. and the downtown was smaller than my neighborhood shopping district of Chelten and Germantown Avenues. Book People, a funky bookstore, stood out as the bus drove along the Worcester Commons.

Book People had a large sign with a yellow back ground and multiple colored letters. It was a symbolic clash of cultures that represented in a small way the youth movement/hippie movement. At a later date Abbie Hoffman returned to his home in Worcester and had a book signing at Book People for his book "Steal this Book". Some kids actually stole several copies and as they ran off Hoffman yelled at them not to steal the book.

The term "commons" and other regional words like "Spa" were then foreign and it took me a while to grasp the colloquialism of the Worcesterites. I took a taxi with my one tightly packed suit case to the College. After signing in at Hogan Center I was assigned a room on the first floor of Carlin Dorm. At that time it was an older freshmen dorm; today it has been converted to prized senior suites.

Then it was the policy of the College that all of the Black students be assigned White roommates. The White roommates had been asked if they wanted to share a room with a Black student, but no Black student was asked if he wanted to share a room with a White student. It was rumored that in a previous class a White student walked out of his room assignment when he saw his Black roommate. The College wanted to prevent a repeat of such an incident.

Fred was my roommate, the son of an oil executive. Fred was daring, but not political as he did not have much to say about the historical events taking place around him. We cut down a Christmas tree from the College grounds in December 1968, made crank calls, and got drunk together. He was fun to be with and he seemed to accept me as a friend. He did one thing that I later regretted. Fred put a Nazi flag his dad brought back from World War II on the ceiling of our room. When we spoke about it, he said that it was a novelty and showed the defeat of the Nazis. I realize now it was plain offensive and I should have told him to take it down.

Fred and the other kids on Carlin first floor were good kids when it came to helping others. A non-student activist from Worcester, Richard Brovensi, was fundraising for a charity and he asked me if some of the kids from my dorm could help out. Richard had worked a deal with a traveling carnival in which the tickets proceeds would be shared if he could provide help with ticket sellers for the booths. Five of us from Carlin and Ed from Beaven Dorm volunteered.

I remember Ron selling a ticket at the carnival to a Puerto Rican woman and the police arrested her. They said she was intoxicated. I never saw her drink and when she separated from her friends the police cuffed her. I was very upset and I asked

Ron what had happened. He said that he would not had sold her a ticket if he had known she was drunk. I almost yelled at him because I thought the cops were racists and that the woman was not drunk. I caught myself and told him that he did nothing wrong and I was happy he helped out. This incident gave credibility at the time to the Panthers' slogan of "off the pigs". It was a step to my radicalization. A week later Richard brought a case of ale to my room and I invited everyone on the corridor to the ale to thank them for their help.

To my surprise, shortly after moving into Carlin, I realize there was a Black student assigned to the room next door. Gil was also from Philadelphia. I found out he was dating a girl, Cathy, with whom I had gone to grammar school. I used to call him "Cathy's clown" after a pop song. I liked Gil a lot as we could fool around and he never got angry. Sadly he died in an accident in the early 1990's. .

***

September of 1968 was idyllic. Classes had just started and as far as we knew we were all academically safe. The weather that late summer was warm and ideal for the intramural freshman football played on the freshmen fields located at the bottom of College Hill. During one of the games I suffered a fairly deep cut in my hand while breaking my fall. The whole team stopped playing, forfeiting the game and took me to the nurse's office.

When we got there we must have been a sight. My sweat shirt was covered in blood and there were seven students surrounding me. The nurse asked us as we entered the door way,

"Is this some sort of prank?" When she saw the cut she cleaned it and called for security to take me to St. Vincent Hospital, then located on Vernon Hill.

At the hospital it was decided that stitches were required. Before the procedure began a novice nun from Ireland and I began to talk. I believed that she felt obliged to talk as a part of her duty. She spoke with a really heavy, but pleasant to hear, accent. She asked me what happened and how I fell returning a kickoff. I could tell she was nervous and shy, but she listened quite intently to a description of a game she probably knew very little about.

While the doctor stitched my hand; he said that he was going to leave the stitches loose so that any dirt that might be in the wound would be able to migrate out. He said there would be a scar. I still have that scar today.

When I went to the lobby, I could not find the officer who drove me to the hospital. So I decided to walk back to the College. You could actually see the College from Vernon Hill. I just walked in that direction asking people as I went along. I saw the officer later and he said I should have called him. I did not bother to tell him I did not know the phone number.

The campus security found itself, probably unjustly, the target of student anger. Several times during the snowy months kids would begin to throw snow balls at the officer's traffic shack in front of O'Kane. The officers were pinned inside for a while until they warned the kids that other officers were on their way.

When we did not throw snowballs at the officers we would throw them at each other. There was a big snowball fight between Carlin and Alumni dorms. Alumni dorm was directly across the Quad. As an eighteen year old my sight was better than today and I worked out. This allowed me to throw a snow ball with relative accuracy. As some Alumni kids tried to flank us I hit each one with a snow ball and hit the lead kid twice. He then yelled out that he was being "creamed" and retreated. The others soon followed.

I grew tired of the snowball fight and made my way back to my room. The next day I heard some of the Carlin kids say they lost the fight and were driven back into the building.

***

We formed the Black Student Union (BSU) that Fall and at first it seemed to be only a social club, organizing mixers, and getting more Black students to attend Holy Cross. There was no social event on campus at which we felt entirely comfortable. The BSU provided a means to have some control over our social lives. At first it was just going to different colleges and meeting the other Black students in New England. This was especially true for the women colleges where the Black students were as isolated as we were. One of our outings was to Smith College. There was a female student who came over to me and was sociable. I was cordial, but did not want to spend time with her as she was heavy set. After a few words I excused myself. To this day I regretted I was so shallow and worse. I was so obviously shallow.

During the summer of 1970 I took a course at Temple University and I met a lady student who was also heavy set. She was cute so I asked her out. She said OK, but she never said when we could go out. I liked her more than she liked me. It made me realize I was presumptuous at Smith.

That social club perspective of the BSU quickly changed when Bob, a Black sophomore from Savannah GA, asked at a BSU meeting for us to go to the main Worcester Police station to protest the police beating of a Black Worcester teenager, Patty. Perry gave an awful, but irrefutable speech in support of the protest. It was awful because it did not raise the protest in terms of civil rights and the struggle against racism. He instead asked us to imagine Patty as our respective kid sister beaten by the police. After the meeting we headed to the main Worcester Police Station on Waldo St. near the County Jail on Summer St. They were both in the mostly Black neighborhood of Laurel-Clayton. Sixteen of us marched into the police station.

Bob and others began a dialog with the cops inside. After listening for a while I went outside and stood by the front door. In Philly I would run from the cops and going into a police station is still hard

Patty went to court and was found guilty. The police officers who used excessive force were cleared.

***

The year 1968 was an election year. President Johnson chose not to run again for President of the United States because of the anti war opposition around the country. Hubert Horatio Humphrey became the nominee of the Democratic Party. He was for civil rights and against poverty and that was good enough for me. I did not fully understand the significance of the police riot during the Democratic Convention and the Vietnam War.

In 1968 eighteen year olds could not vote, but I volunteered at the Humphrey Office in Worcester. The office was located in downtown Worcester on Main Street near the Denholms Building, a busy place then that has since fallen on hard times. Two woman students from Clark University also were there on the day I volunteered. A middle age campaign worker welcomed us and made us listen to the Rascals' ""People Got to Be Free". After which he gave a little speech about Humphrey. It was embarrassing. However I took some flyers and a button.

Craig, had become something of a cultural political guru on the campus. He questioned me about my Humphrey button. I told Craig I thought he was a phony. It took me a while to acknowledge he had a better insight into the politics of the elections than I did.

It was in New Haven during a demonstration to Free the Black Panthers organized by a variety of groups that I have my most vivid memory of Craig. A battle broke out between the police and the anarchists or Yippies as some were then known. Rev. Slaoan-Coflin, the chaplain at Yale University, gathered about him several pacifists and did the police's job. He and they swept the street of the rebels. I would think about this when I heard the lament about some pacifists "they don't fight, but when they do fight they fight the communists". Among the pacifists was Craig. He and I were both stunned to see the other. I thought that he knew better than to do the cop's job. He did not think I would be among the rebels. Even though we would see each other off and on until 1972, we never spoke of those events in New Haven.

***

John was a community organizer while in high school, running programs for working class kids in Bridgeport Connecticut. He continued to do so when he got to Holy Cross through Student Program Urban Development (SPUD). I went to a SPUD organized event at the Boys Club on Ionic Ave. The Boys and Girl Club has since moved to Tainter St. The kids at the Boys Club were mostly White and they did not look poor. This was a surprise to me. I had been a Big Brother at Cardinal Dougherty and the kids I worked with were from North Philly and they were Black and mostly poor.

I found it hard to imagine that White people outside of Appalachia could be poor. It was a misconception I got from "The Other America" and television documentaries. I was faced with a moral dilemma that I still confront today. When faced with two sets of poor people one White and one Black which group do you spend time and organize?

After the event I told John I did not feel right working with the White kids when I knew there were Black kids in Worcester who needed my help. I could tell by John's voice that I disappointed him greatly. He pled with me and argued with me, but I made a decision based on what I felt at the time. I can see now it was the wrong decision. It was not too much later I came to the realization that poor people regardless of their origins have much in common and that I was wrong consciously picking one group over another. It was for this reason that I would later work with Ed and the Free Breakfast for Children Program even though the kids were mostly White. It is still a question that bothers me because of the added road blocks faced by dark skin people in the USA and around the world.

Chapter 3
Thumb Out

The 1960's presented us with what seemed to be proof that somehow the fundamental nature of humans had changed without the material conditions around us changing. During my high school years there were a be-in in Rittenhouse Square, a love-in at Fairmount Park, and psychedelic music concerts in JFK stadium.

When I got to Holy Cross I felt that the culture had changed significantly and by living this new culture others would change. Somehow this state of mind translated into a concept of hitching being a safe thing to do.

My first hitchhiking adventure was in the Fall of 1968. I was homesick. It was overwhelming like a physical illness. When I worked at Holy Cross in 2005 a woman student faced homesickness similar to my own; the Bishop Healy Committee of the Alumni Association gave her money to return home for a week. She returned to College and made a very good adjustment.

One Saturday in October 1968 I walked up onto I 290 West and held out my thumb. Getting a ride from I 290 to the Mass Pike and then to the Sturbridge entrance of I 84 was fairly easy. Once on I 84 I began to have second thoughts. Hours seem to go by without anyone stopping and I was afraid I would be caught out on a highway at night.

An old beat up Plymouth eventually stopped and it was filled with people. There was barely enough room for me to fit in the back seat. The driver asked me where I was going and I said "Philadelphia". He did not say any thing after that. None of the other people in the car said anything either. We just silently rode down I 84 until the driver suddenly stopped near Hartford and two people got out. They thanked the driver and then walked down the exit. Not too far from the junction with Route 15 the driver pulled over and picked up another hitchhiker. Then I realized that the driver was picking up every hitchhiker on the road if he had room. He let me off near New Haven.

Around 3 PM a middle age man driving a Cadillac stopped. I always thought that people driving Cadillacs were show offs or worse, but I was not going to turn down a ride. He said he was drowsy and he wanted me to drive while he took a nap. I drove along I 95 in the Cadillac with the sleeping man until we came to a construction area. The traffic backed up. We inched along through the construction when the engine stalled. This happens sometimes on stick shift cars. I tried to restart the engine as the car in front of me pulled away. Standing in the road was a Connecticut State Trooper waving at me to get the car moving. At this point the middle age guy woke. He said to be calm and just drive. The car jerked forward and then we were passed. I thought the Trooper would pull us over as he must have seen a teenage Black kid driving a Cadillac with a weary eye White man. Once out of sight of the Trooper the middle age man told me to pull over at a safe location as he wanted to drive. I asked if he was still sleepy and he said that the twenty minute nap was enough for him to be alert. We drove over the George Washington Bridge and he let me off at the entrance of the New Jersey Turnpike (NJTP). I wondered if I could catch another ride before dark.

Just as I was walking over to the side of the toll booths to show the traffic my sign reading "Philadelphia", a New Jersey State Trooper who was parked off to the side began rolling towards me. I thought I was going to jail as hitchhiking was illegal on the NJTP. Incredibly a car pulled in front of the State Police car and the driver opened his door and said "get in".

The driver was a business man and he was heading to Philadelphia Airport to pickup a woman associate who was flying in from Europe. He was already late. He picked me up because he thought that I knew how to get to the Airport from the turnpike. Of course I said that I did. As he drove he talked a little about himself, his company, and that it was likely his friend would be in the bar waiting for him. I was only half listening as I was trying to think about the exit for the Airport. When we came to Exit 6 "Penna. Turnpike" he asked if that was the right way. I said that I thought it was, but I was not sure.

At the toll booths near the Delaware River the driver ask for directions to the Philadelphia Airport and he was told that the best way was to get back on the NJTP and get off at the Walt Whitman bridge. I was a little embarrassed.

We did not talk much the rest of way. I was dropped off at the terminal and took a taxi to 30th Station and then took the train to Germantown and home. Although hitchhiking to Philadelphia was not as easy as I first thought it gave me confidence that I could hitchhike anywhere and a sense of independence. It meant that I could get home anytime I wanted and a sense of no longer being isolated on campus.

My parents were surprised to see me and adamant that I not hitchhike back. My dad the next day drove me to the bus station, paid for my ticket, and watched me leave for Worcester for the second time in a little over a month. He must have known then that Holy Cross and I were a difficult fit.

***

At one of the Holy Cross mixers in Freshman year I met a girl from Iran. She was a student at Annhurst College in Connecticut, a Catholic college for women; it is now closed. We exchanged addresses and I forgot about her until I noticed a poster for a mixer at Annhurst. I decided to go and look her up. I had to first find the town in Connecticut on a map to determine what my signs would read and how many were needed. The town was Woodstock on Route 44. I needed two signs with different highway numbers and one with the town name.

The trip was so uneventful that I only remember the last driver went a bit out of his way to take me to Woodstock. The trip took only a few hours and it was about 2:00 PM when I arrived. The mixer was at 7:00 PM so I had to spend some time in town.

It was a really small town which you could walk end to end in about forty minutes or less. I know this because I walked it end to end. While walking I would look at the ground to search for coins that people may have dropped. I walked up a small street while looking down and when I looked up there was a train station with about twenty White people staring at me. I must had been a sight for them, a Black man on foot walking through their town and walking straight toward them. If there were only one or two White people I would have said hello and left. However this time I looked at them for a few seconds and turned around. I saw a donut shop and went inside to get something to eat and to regain my composure. Afterward I went into a book store and bought a book on mixed marriages. I read about half the book before starting my walk to the college.

The college was three or four miles outside of town on Route 44. I thought about hitching a ride, but I decided to just walk, as it was getting dark and a car stopping for me after the sun had gone done was unlikely.

I went to the girl's dorm and ask the student at the desk to see the Iranian girl. When she came down from her room we talked a while in the lobby about her and Iran. She was sociable, but it was clear that she was not interested in me. I told her that I was going to the mixer and then said good bye. Sometimes I wonder what happened to her, especially after the Shah was overthrown.

The mixer was anti climatic as I spent my time trying to get a ride back to Holy Cross. Ironically, instead of talking with girls I asked guys if they were from Holy Cross. I lucked out and one guy said he was and would give me a ride back. His girl friend went to the college and he was not planning to leave until her curfew. However I was happy to get a ride back.

***

Regis College was the official sister college to Holy Cross, as Holy Cross was all male and Regis College was all women; the women cheerleaders at the football games were from Regis. It was not clear why Anna Maria College in Paxton was not officially the sister college as it was only 10 miles away. There were maybe eight or ten Black women students at Regis in 1968. In later years the number of Black women students would increase and include my buddy Al's girlfriend from Georgia, Ouivonida. I remember how Al complained that his girlfriend's classmates said that she should dump him because he wasn't good enough for her.

One of the upper class women student, Shelly, was strikingly beautiful. She and her friends met with some of us and we made plans to collaborate on activities.

One of the activities was a discussion at Regis on race relations. The talk did not go well as the divide between White and Black students actually became worse. There were no experienced moderators at this event who could have smoothed over points of division. I told Shelly how sorry I was that the discussion did not turn out to be more of a positive experience. She said that it was useful and that it would generate further talks.

I think it was Spring 1969 when Shelly sent me a letter inviting the Black men in the BSU to a mixer at Regis. I made the membership aware of it, but there did not seem to be much interest. I could not even get the BSU to let me use the BSU van to drive to Regis. Without the van there was no way to get anyone else to go. I really liked Shelly and I felt obliged to go. So I decided to hitch hike.

To get to Regis was fairly straight forward. It was in Wellesley close to Route 9. The trip started with the walk from Holy Cross to Lincoln Square, a heavily travelled rotary in Worcester on Route 9 that no longer exists today. Leaving around three PM, I thought that I had plenty of time before the sun went down.

Being it was a Saturday night, I did not have much trouble getting rides going down Route 9. A lot of idealistic young kids like me were driving about. The last driver even drove me to Regis as I told him that I did not have a clue how to get there from the Route 9 exit.

The mixer was a disappointment. Shelly asked about Ted and Eddie, two football players. She asked where were the other Black men. Although we were friends, it became clear soon enough that I did not have a chance with her romantically. I stayed only long enough to get something to eat as I knew it was going to be tough getting back to my dorm.

I asked some kids about how to get to Route 9, but their instructions were confusing. They had driven to Regis and so they gave non pedestrian instructions. I got lost right away and I must have walked around for several hours until a car stopped and a man in his thirties asked me if I needed a ride. Cold and tired, I said yes.

We began to talk and I told him I went to Regis to see my girlfriend. He said that I must be in love to have gone through so much trouble. I didn't answer and the subject changed. Somehow the driver started talking about watching pornographic movies. This subject caught me off guard and I began to wonder if I was in danger. However we soon came to the Junction of Route 126 and Route 9 in Framingham. I thanked the driver and began to look for a ride west on Route 9.

It was still dark and few cars were on the road. But soon the sun came up and I finally caught a ride, getting back to campus about 10 AM. I headed to my dorm and went to sleep, just a little wiser about how things worked. That was the last time I hitched hike to see a girl.

***

I am not sure how I met Annie. She was a nurse from Tennessee. I can say that this was not love at first sight, but she had a pleasant personality. She and her older sister Liz had recently moved to Worcester and were staying with their cousin who lived off of Healy Road in Worcester.

Our first date was a mixer in Carlin Dorm. We danced a little and talked a lot. I remember a dorm mate named Bif (I am not kidding) coming over. He would call the females "girlies" I was hoping he would not embarrass me. He just made small talk and then left.

After several dates (Ho Toy, Green Hill Park, and David Ruffin without the Temptations) it became clear that Annie and I liked Liz more than we liked each other. Liz came with us on our dates either as tag along or double date with her boyfriend. One time we went into Roxbury to see Annie's other sister, Jackie. Jackie was married to an Ethiopian man. When we picked Jackie up someone started to follow us with their headlights off and he eventually made us pull to the side of the road. I thought it was the cops. It was instead Jackie's husband who said he wanted to find out where his wife was going.

On another date we went to one of Annie's White friend's house party. One of the things I learned quickly when coming to New England was that when Black people had a party there was soul music and dancing and for White people there was elevator music and no dancing. Annie, Liz, and I sat near the record player. After a while I said to Annie that we should put on James Brown and dance. She was reluctant, saying it was not proper. I did it anyway and we got up to dance. To our surprise everyone else at the party also began to dance. I thought that the change would be for the rest of the party, but Annie became angry when I tried a second time. I relented and just talked for the rest of the party.

We dated long enough that her cousin told one of the Deans at Holy Cross we were engaged. It's ironic that when the Dean mentioned it to me, I had already broken up with Annie.

Annie's cousin had a three year old daughter, Penny, who knew Annie's middle name, Maude. Annie never wanted me to know her middle name and she bribed her cousin to keep it a secret. In the 1980s I saw Penny in the newspaper as a Black debutante.

Chapter 4
Bible Studies

The College of the Holy Cross was in flux in 1968 as well as was most of the world. Mandatory mass was abolished the year before. During Freshman year I went to mass several times, but it was not like going to mass with my relatives and friends in Philadelphia. Doug, a friend in grammar school, and I would go to the 7 AM mass with our fishing poles and then walk over to Wissahickon Creek to catch the stocked trout. To a significant degree the parish church and its members kept me a Catholic. Coming to Holy Cross gave me an opportunity to realize the connection between belief and social activity.

At some point it became clear that the mass and other Church events at my parish were the glue that kept my friends and relatives connected. My friends' parents and my mom knew each other and socialized at the church's events. We went as families to mass. We all had something in common to speak about when we met. This experience I thought was the love of God. At Holy Cross I found that my love of my family and friends was not the same as love of God. Even though I initially went to mass at Holy Cross it did not fill the void of missing my family and friends.

I would search in many places to find something that could fill that void. Ironically my experiences at Holy Cross has led me to find a separation between duty to humans and duty to God. After a while the assertion of the connection of duty to God and duty to humans could not be sustained. I had lost faith. The duty to humans was compelling and the duty to God became an individual's choice.

***

What had not changed much at Holy Cross in 1968 were the requirements for a degree, although these too would later change. The conventional wisdom was to get all of the requirements out of the way in Freshman and Sophomore years. At the time a religious course was needed and I took Bible Studies in the Fall of 1968. I rarely went to that class. Possibly it reminded me of the classes on Catholicism at Cardinal Dougherty. Even if I had written good test essays, no professor would have given me a passing grade, given the missed classes. Having failed Bible Studies I knew that my QPA would never be good no matter what I did afterwards. However I went into the Spring of 1969 with resolve to get my QPA up. I retook Bible Studies with the same professor. I attended more classes than the semester before and received a passing grade.

I came to realized that studying the Bible was a meaningless activity for me at the time. I have recently found it useful when arguing with fundamentalists. I tell them that the Bible is archaic and cannot be used for ethical living in today's society. I refer them to the story of Samson who killed three hundred people in another tribe (genocide?) because someone played a joke on him.

The professor of Bible Studies rarely spoke to me, although other students said he was quite sociable. One day he said that he was glad that someone was sensible and did not go to the GE protest. I did not respond as I had no idea what he was talking about. After class his words became clearer. He was referring to the blockade of the Student Center steps preventing the GE recruiters from entering Hogan. GE had made the delivery systems for napalm (a weapon that many thought should be banned.) The blockade of the steps was organized by the Revolutionary Students Union (RSU) and four Black students joined in: Al, Jeff, Perry, and Craig. When it became known that they were to be expelled an emergency meeting of the BSU was called.

Chapter 5
Why Are We Going Back?

The Black Student Union (BSU) was the first of what are now called ALANA (Asian Latino, Afro American, Native American) groups at Holy Cross. The ALANA groups now include women, Mixed, and Gay-Lesbians. Although mixed race, I am Black .When I worked at Holy Cross I found myself attending Mixed meeting to hear how the students dealt with being mixed race.

The BSU was formed in 1968 when twenty five Black Students entered Holy Cross in the Class of 1972. That was thought to be a sufficient numbers to have a vital and sustainable organization. There was a general consensus that Art would be the President of the BSU. Being a senior he knew the College better than most of us and he had contacts with the administration. The thing I remember most about Art was that he could talk, small talk or profound speeches. He was able to hold the BSU together and guide it through its formative year. It was his idea to walk out of school, when the four Black students were expelled for blocking the GE recruiters. He was on the negotiating team that dealt with the administration.

Art was able to articulate the theoretical basis for the racism of the expulsion of the four Black students. All of the Black students participating in the GE protest were expelled and only some of the White students were expelled. There was a disparity in the way the students to be expelled were chosen.

On the day we walked out some of us gathered at Art's room and turned on his roommate's stereo and we began to party in the corridor. His White roommate complained that the loudness of the music had damaged his speakers. Art promised to replace them. I thought it to be a curious gesture as we were walking out of College possibly never to return.

In 2006 my buddy Darrell provided me some photos of the walkout and the BSU members entering vehicles to exit the campus. There was a gathering of Black students at Hogan Campus Center ball room, where they throw down their IDs and left campus. Most of us rode the BSU van and stayed near Clark University.

I remember we walked out on a Friday and we agreed to stay near campus until the negotiating team talked with the administration. On Sunday we had a meeting with a potential mediator from Worcester named John Scott. He was a light skin Black psychologist. He died recently. One of the students, Mike, thought he was White and challenged his being at the meeting.

After Jack Scott made his presentation he asked us what did we want to do and expect to happen. Several of the students wanted to return to the College with no conditions. They felt that they had done enough. It seemed to me that all that we did would be for nothing if we returned without something. I spoke. I asked the rhetorical question "If we left due to racism, why are we going back to the College?" The tone of the discussion changed. I remember Jaffe saying that we should not go back to the College and so it was agreed that we not return unless the four expelled students were readmitted. I believe that the next Tuesday we received word that the College agreed to our conditions.

The return was full of mixed emotion. The IDs that were thrown down a few days earlier were in the mailboxes on our return. We who took part in the walk out had bonded. I am still saddened that Clarence has renounced this event. The walk out had split the College. More students, faculty, and administration supported us than did not. Those who did not, became hardened in their views. There is an ironic twist to our walking out of College, the four Black students we help to return to the College later left the College on their own or due to academics.

***

When Art graduated a competition grew between Ted and Clarence for the Presidency of the BSU. It was not obvious to me at first there was even a behind the scenes struggle. There were differences in opinions. One of the differences was how the money for the BSU was to be spent. I had raised in a meeting that a lady from Worcester was in need of help and that the BSU could set aside some money as a donation. The item was voted down, but Clarence sided with me.

I do not remember clearly the election of Ted as President of the BSU. I remember there was some controversy and animosity about the election. Because of the animosity I began to visit some of the BSU members outside of the meetings. While talking with Clarence he said that he hated Ted's policies. Things settled down and we all remained in the organization.

Some in the BSU thought that I was siding with Clarence and criticized me for visiting BSU members and talking policy outside of the meeting. I was surprised that anyone thought that I had so much influence. Until the time I left the College there was a love hate relationship between me and some of the BSU officers.

***

A couple of incidents stand out in my mind that happened during BSU meetings. The first incident was Clarence standing up in a meeting and announcing that he could see a Black woman student walking hand in hand across the Hogan parking lot with a White male student. Some of us got up and looked from the window. I felt uncomfortable as I was from a racially mixed marriage. The meeting went off topic as we argued about the suitableness of mixed race marriages.

The woman was a student from Regis College whom I had gone to see during one of my hitchhiking adventures. Today I don't understand what was going through Clarence's mind when he stood up and pointed to Shelly with a White male friend.

The other incident makes me want to crawl into a shell even today. In theory the BSU was not just a Black student group, but it was open to students of all races. However no White person dared join. A Palestinian student named Michael joined. He came to every meeting and he sympathized with the civil rights movement and he sought our help with the occupation of Palestine by Israel.

He was tolerated by some, but I felt he was my friend. The Black Muslims students led a group that forced him out of the BSU. They considered Michael to be White even though he was Muslim in his beliefs. There was a meeting in which Dean, one of the Black Muslim students, said unkind things about Michael. Several students including myself defended Michael. No vote was taken, but after the meeting Michael resigned his membership. This was an injustice I could not fix even though it should had been fixable.

***

The walkout helped to give Holy Cross a reputation as a radical school. Some magazine voted the College as the most radical college in New England in 1970. Sometime shortly after the walkout the Clark University BSU took over the Clark University Administration building. The Black students there asked us to help. It was decided that the Holy Cross Black students would remain outside of the door way leading to the building. The thinking was that we would discourage any attempts to forcefully end the take over by police or right wing students. So we stood outside in the rain for eight hours. Finally someone from the inside said we should go get something to eat. Which was welcomed and we would bring back some food for the Clark students. When we got back the Clark students had left the building, saying that they had reached an agreement with the administration. We did not see how this was possible, but we did not care so much as most of us did not want to stand in the rain through the night. I joked with Steve and Cheez that we were not keeping the cops out of the building as much as we were keeping the Clark students in.

Chapter 6
Alienation Free Zones

Being away at college is an alienating experience. You are separated from all that is familiar and the class and race divisions become more profound. The competitive environment of academia can also be alienating. Some of the nastier fights are over seemingly insignificant minutia. A White freshman classmate from the Detroit area transferred after the first semester with a cumulative average of 4.0 to Wayne State. He said that the environment at Holy Cross was wrong for him and he could be more of a person at a state college.

Being a Black kid growing up in a city like Philadelphia you had to learn to become multi—cultural, if you wanted to succeed. You had to learn the culture of minority and majority populations. I acted and spoke differently in each cultural. The White kids would complain about us Black kids not being truthful as they noticed that we acted differently in different cultural settings. When in high school it was easy to separate the two ways of doing things; we Black kids sat together at lunch and stayed together at the dances.

The dances at Cardinal Dougherty High School were segregated. Black boys danced with Black girls. We always went to the farthest corner from the door. I suppose our nascent feeling of nationalism played a role. There were also other forces at work, the racial mores of Philadelphia and the country. The city neighborhoods were in transition. My parents moved from a mostly Black neighborhood in West Philadelphia to the mostly White neighborhood of Germantown. The changes to the neighborhoods did not always go smoothly and there was racial tension. Dancing with some one of another race drew stares. Even though everyone had friends of different races, interracial dating was still something of a taboo.

Dating has been problematic for Black students at Holy Cross. It was so during my freshman year and is still so, especially for the Black women students.

In 1968 Holy Cross' mixers were quite new to me. I was literally outside of my social constraints of Philadelphia. I would go to the mixers and dance with anyone I wanted. Although the mixers were fun, I can't think of one Black student who ever dated a White girl he met at a mixer.

I went to the mixers with James who was a good buddy at the time. He was fun to be around and he was candid about race. Being from Washington DC, the urban South, he brought a new and different perspective than that I had grown to know in Philadelphia. It was from Jim that I heard for the first time the following observation on race.

Yellow good fellow
Brown stick around
Black stay back

Jimmy and I became roommates on the Black corridor in the Fall of 1969. Unfortunately we had a falling out and I have not spoken to him since then.

***

In college it was hard to escape the politics of race, because we could not easily escape the college environment and the politics of integration and separation. This criticism of us Black kids was one of the primary reasons we chose to create and form the Black Corridor in Bishop Healy dorm. We could be Black without apology. I remember a heated discussion in my dorm room between a group of White students and Walter and me, about integration. It was going nowhere and I became frustrated. Walter had an insight which changed the direction of the discussion. He said that white skin allowed White people to be more easily judged by their character than their race. The implication is that the integration of the melting pot theory for race relations was flawed.

Although the issue of race sometimes is suppressed and the conditions seem to be neutral the issue reappears in unexpected forms. The Black Corridor in Healy dorm was not entirely Black as several of the Black students had White roommates from their freshman year. One of the lessons learned from living on the Black Corridor is that conditions compelled us to interact with the other students on campus. The Black Corridor was a means to integration, one of several options. For some of us the Black corridor helped to alleviate the alienation.

At the football games we Black kids sat together. Many of us did not go to the football games because the College song included the lyrics "Old Black Joe". Some of us went to see Eddie, Jaffe, and the other Black players.

Few Black kids stood for the national anthem. It was partly due to the racism in the USA and the Vietnam War, but it was also due to the fact that we had to a certain extent grown beyond nationalism and allegiance to any state. We had become internationalists, identifying with the struggles around the world and holding a vision beyond the jurisdiction of any set of borders.

Today I give the respect to those who are nationalists and follow their customs. However like many churches and religious groups, I can not pledge allegiance to any nation state. Once you have grown in beliefs there is no ungrowing Today there are people who see the Black Corridor as only an issue of separation. It was actually an issue of haven. Most of the colleges in the country at the time had their equivalent of a Black corridor. I understand today that there are few colleges with Black corridors options.

There were some problems living on the Black Corridor, but my good experiences outweighed the bad. I remember the chess games; I was always looking for good competition especially from the incoming classes. There was the sharing of music, especially the tapes of the radio stations in Philly, WDAS and WHAT. They were soul music stations and I longed for Philly when I heard the tapes. For a while I imagined I was at home and then became sad when the tape ended.

In Massachusetts then, there was only one soul music station, WILD which had a weak signal and went off the air at sundown. Today I am happy for internet radio as there are still few R & B stations in New England.

Steve and John would often get a group of us to go over to the field house and play in the pick up basketball games. I did not play as it seemed that they took the game too seriously. They would come back and be banged up with some interesting story about payback the next day.

Enjoyable were the parties we had on the Corridor. Black students from other colleges would come and socialize in the hallways of our dorm. There was food, beverage and music. We opened up our dorm rooms or closed them depending on the situation. At one of the dances a woman student from Atlantic Union and I were socializing in my dorm. I had no roommate at that time. After a while I realized how conservative the Seventh Day Adventists were. In a short while she rejoined her friends in the corridor.

One evening on the Corridor Wizard and his buddies played a clever prank. After the cafeteria in Hogan closed for the night the College allowed a pizza franchise to go through the dorms selling pizza. Students did the actual selling and they usually sold out of pizza fairly quickly each night.

When moving down the halls of the dorms, the student sellers would drag or push their boxes of pizzas and yell out "pizza, hot pizza". Wizard got a box filled with junk and kicked it down the corridor, yelling "Pizza, Hot Pizza". A lot of kids including myself opened our doors thinking the pizza man was there; Wizard had a good laugh, but he didn't stay long enough to hear what we thought about the prank. Afterward when the pizza man came we never were quite sure he was not Wizard.

Wizard was not the only prankster. Around this time Listerine came out with plastic bottles, replacing glass. As this was not well known I throw the plastic bottle on the floor of Tank's dorm room. Tank was a kid from the Bronx. He jumped back thinking that the glass would break. We had a good laugh. He then said we should do this to the guys on the Corridor. Everyone laughed each time we did. However the last laugh was on me as the plastic bottle sprang a leak and I lost its contents without ever using it.

Clarence was fun to be around when he was around. He spent most of his time in the stacks of the library. He would make it a point to be talkative and he would tell jokes like only he could tell. The two that stand out are his joke about Black men from the South eating ham and having penises so long that they had to strap them to their legs. The other was about a coke can with pubic hair. I had no idea what the coke can joke was about or why would pubic hairs be on a coke can. It is still a mystery to me.

In my senior year Clarence visited after he had enrolled in Yale Law School. At the time Clarence dressed like a Black Panther wannabe with the fatigues, boots, and beret. He said that he had gone to the desk to register for the law courses when the lady behind the desk said that Clarence should go to the other building for the inner city kids. After explaining that he was a law student did the lady allow him to register. We told him that it might be time to get new clothes.

Clarence had what I thought then was a credible explanation for the cause of female homosexuality. He thought that women became homosexuals because of sustained mistreatment by men. He would mention it several times when criticizing the mistreatment of Black women. Given the misconceptions of the times I thought it made sense for some time afterwards.

In spite of the good experiences I had with Cooz I feel betrayed by him. He, like all of us, was helped by Affirmative Action. He received a Holy Cross scholarship, he recruited Black students to Holy Cross, got into Yale with race based admission policies, and was pick for the Supreme Court to take Justice Marshall former seat. His rulings that cut off this road to success that he took are sad. I said as much when I saw him in 2004.

Eddie who was a star on the football team was a hard guy to figure out. First and foremost he was a jock and a big man on campus. He had groupies around him and never wanted for a date. I was certainly envious. When there were parietals he and some female friends would break them on a regular basis. There was one particular story that James swore was true about Eddie and a student from Clark University that had me rolling in laughter and the thought of what he said still brings a smile to me. It was about a sexual act between Eddie and the Clark student that I have been advised to leave out of this story. There were other times that Eddie would impress me, such as when he went into a gas station identified himself and the owner gave him free gas.

Eddie used to call me "Mexican" because I wore a mustache at the time. However I can't say I always liked his company. He used to tell me that the some young ladies thought I was" not cool". I had no way of knowing whether what he said was true, just meanness, or both.

When the football team was sickened with hepatitis during our Sophomore year Eddie and Jaffe began arguing about a garment that Eddie needed. Jaffe essentially told him to get lost. Then I saw signs of vulnerability on Eddie face as he almost began to beg. At that time I saw just another guy in spite of his trappings of importance. Even though Eddie and I have been in the Boston area since his graduation. I have not felt compelled to look him up.

In 1972 Eddie was drafted by the Miami Dolphins who were undefeated that season. Eddie suffered a broken ankle during the season and he did not play in the Super Bowl. He did manage to get on TV standing in the stadium runway welcoming his victorious team mates. I thought to myself that it was just like Eddie, not in the game but involved enough to get on TV.

***

At my high school in Philadelphia there were not many Black kids. I understand that the Parochial schools in Philly are less segregated now. What the Parochial schools and the Public schools had in common then and I guess now is that almost all the students were working class kids. One of the tougher adjustments at Holy Cross was getting use to the rich kids. I did not understand them and I resented their privilege. I know that they did not understand me and the rich kids that I befriended more or less hid their wealth. I resented their trips to Europe, their cars, their polo playing, and their connections.

I used my fists almost every day in grammar school. If you did not fight, you were bullied. In high school there was less opportunity to fight and my last fight was in Sophomore year. We took it down to the railroad station platform which was mostly empty during the day. I was surprised by how many kids showed up to see me get my ass kicked. I supposed they were disappointed when we throw a couple of punches and then the other guy just quit saying that I "wasn't worth the effort". However no other student at high school confronted me again.

I had a little juice and besides we were trying to prove we were lovers. I tried to impress girls with my dance steps, which were not very good, and with my academic skills, which impressed almost no teenage girl.

Regrettably my bad trait of using my fists popped up again at Holy Cross. It got so bad that when Al sold me his pocket knife, someone on the Corridor stole it from my room. I always thought it was Ted. He was always looking out for us and his taking of my pocketknife was probably in everyone's best interest. Ironically there was a stabbing a year later between two good friends.

I forget what year it was; Vic came back to the corridor and said that some White kid had called him "nigger". After a discussion it was decided that night to pay the kid a visit and demand an apology. As a group we walk to Lehy and bang on the door. When the kid's roommate saw us he left. He must have known what was coming. The kid did not apologize and a scuffle broke out. We broke it up right away and went back to our dorm. Nothing happened afterwards, as I think that the White kid never reported the incident to the administration. I can say that no one ever called us "nigger" after that.

***

There was another place on the campus where I felt comfortable and at home. It was the fourth floor of Fenwick where the Philosophy Department was located. After taking Fr. Diani's Intro to Philosophy in the Spring of 1969 I took as many Philosophy courses as I could. Each philosophical point of view stimulated new questions and an excitement for life. The feeling of journey and discovery shunted aside disagreeable aspects of Holy Cross life and life in general. The top of Fenwick was almost Medieval with odd shapes and wooden panels. There was always hot coffee and a place to sit and read.

Everyone knew my name and I was always welcomed. I would stay there for hours reading and, when the professors were available, discussing issues. There were two professors that helped me to form a coherent point of view from the chaos that surrounded us. Professors Hampsh and Lynch. Dr. Lynch taught logic and Philosophy of Science. Dr. Hampsh was a Trappist monk for twenty-five years and did not speak during that time. He left the brotherhood and became a communist. His explanations of communist theory became the basis of my lifelong study of Marxism- Leninism. We did disagree on how to change history. He supported the German Democratic Republic and was close to the CP USA. I thought the CP USA was a sellout and that German Democratic Republic and the Soviet Union were state capitalist countries and not at all communist.

Dr. Hampsh did me a great favor. I supposed he might have grown tired of listening to a student who knew very little, but insisted on acting like an expert. He said I should give a talk about my ideas. I agreed. I really worked hard to make a good presentation to the many professors, but they methodically asked questions that I could not defend or even answer.

Those professors are deceased now, but I think of them every day as I still ponder philosophical issues. The Philosophy Department today has moved from Fenwick to a new building, Smith, on campus. When I went to the new building I did not get the feeling of a place of learning and questioning, but that of an office building or hospital. It was hard to get used to seeing professors who were younger than me. I am sure that the students are well served by the present day Philosophy Department; I still long for Fenwick 4.

Chapter 7
Inflation and Unemployment

There was no more transformative class than Economics 102 for shaping my life. What I learned shook my fundamental understanding of the world. Unlike philosophy which I enjoyed studying, Economics was dull and unstimulating. After Economics 102 I set out on a path from which I could never return.

The course was taught by Dr. Nordstrom a new professor whose father I would work with years later at US Steel. He would beam with pride when he spoke of his daughter, Dr. Nordstrom. One day in class while we discussed inflation and unemployment. Dr. Nordstrom matter of factly described how an increase in employment caused an increase in inflation. More employment causes more demand and higher prices. So being a true believer in capitalism, I naively asked if you wanted to end poverty with full employment what effect would that have on inflation. Dr. Nordstrom answered that there can never be full employment under capitalism as the inflation would cause the system to go into crisis and break down.

For me it was an epiphany. All of the books about poverty, such as "The Other America" were wrong. Poverty was not due to lack of education or to happenstance. Poverty was an integral part of capitalism. Homelessness, crime, and dependence were symptoms of capitalism not the causes of poverty. My eyes were opened and I felt like I had been lied to and a fool. Capitalism needed poverty in order to function.

My view of racism changed from some bad people holding immoral ideas to racism as a tool to help capitalism. Needing to find alternatives to capitalism I sought out the Marxists. John, a student in the Class of '72, talked about Marxism and through him I came into contact with a Trotskyist group called the Socialist Workers Party (SWP) and their youth group the Young Socialists Alliance (YSA). Nearly forty years later I would again see John in Worcester at the wake for the wife of Frank, an Ex-man of the Class of '72. John who became an attorney in Worcester working in the court system is still a progressive, but I don't think he is a Marxist any longer.

John and I would hitchhike into Boston to go to YSA study groups. He felt that hitchhiking was a waste of time, but we had no other transportation.

I liked the SWP because it was not associated with the Soviet Union; it was Trotskyist. I became disillusioned with SWP after a while as it made identity politics a principle instead of a tactic. It also supported mainstream candidates; none of whom wanted to rid the world of capitalism. Ed, my roommate, told me that a SWP organizer intentionally misstated the races of the four students killed by the National Guard at Kent State.

Afterwards it was logical for me to become more involved in the Revolutionary Student Union (RSU) at Holy Cross which had two students that sort of naturally became its leaders, Bob who later became a conservative Republican, and Ray who is now deceased. Ray would eventually become an advisor to Mayor Kevin White of Boston. Bob became a reporter for the Worcester Telegram.

The members of the RSU reflected the diversity of ideas of the left from pacifism to the Weathermen. We did have some principles in common, a classless society undivided by race or gender and an end to imperialist war. However we differed sharply on tactics. I became more involved with the Worker Student Alliance of SDS and Progressive Labor Party and represented that point of view within the RSU.

***

The relationship between the BSU and the RSU was never formal, but it was symbiotic. The Administration completely ignored the RSU and was quite willing to expel the bunch of us. However the RSU would help the BSU in its struggles. When united, even behind the scenes, the strengths of both organizations were multiplied. The first example of this was the BSU walkout. The event that started the ball rolling was the blocking of the GE recruiters. The walkout strengthened the BSU and allowed the reversal of the expulsion of RSU students as well.

Another example was the Black Panthers from New Haven speaking at Holy Cross. Ray approached me about the Black Panthers. He indicated that the Panthers wanted a two thousand dollar honorarium to speak.

The RSU had no money for speakers. Ray asked me to get the BSU to sponsor the Panthers and pay some of the honorarium. The BSU agreed and the Panthers came for the first and only time to Holy Cross.

The most interesting interaction between the BSU and RSU was the BSU's take over of the administration buildings, in the Spring of 1972. Immediately before the BSU occupied the buildings, the RSU had a sit in at the Naval ROTC offices in O Kane. We did not interfere with the ROTC work, but we did not leave the offices even after closing. We spent the entire night in the office. The administration did not force us to leave. During the RSU sit-in the BSU took over O Kane and Fenwick.

Both the ROTC cadets and the RSU radicals were forced by the BSU to leave. I was allowed to stay, being a BSU member. At that time some in the BSU considered me to be too radical for BSU's image. So I was left out of many of the policy meetings (as were several others). My estrangement from the BSU inner circle was reflected in my assignment during the takeover; it was to guard a chained door far from everyone else. When I worked at Holy Cross in 2005 the sight of that door still evoked strong emotions.

It was never clear to me what the take over was about although I heard Ted and Henry say that the administration was ignoring the demands of the BSU and that negotiations had become stalled. Since I was left out of the loop, I was not even sure there were negotiations. After we left the building there were no clear or tangible results.

I do know that the RSU sit-in emboldened the BSU to take action. When some in the BSU saw the RSU was occupying the Naval ROTC offices with impunity, I am sure it influenced BSU officers' decision for the takeover.

Chapter 8
"Jesuits Off Campus"

The Reserve Officer Training Corp (ROTC) Programs were the target of the anti—war movement at Holy Cross. ROTC contributed to the war in Vietnam. Although some on campus said that the officers from Holy Cross who would served in the military would bring progressive change to it. Subsequent facts showed that the war was unjust and a lie perpetrated on America and the world. The Vietnamese Communists after defeating the Japanese, the French, and the American armies, later overthrow Pol Pot (who was allied with China and the USA) in Cambodia and defended itself against China (supported by the USA) during the1980s. Vietnam does not occupy any country today and is a favored trading partner with the USA. The Vietnam War was unnecessary and I am proud to have opposed it. I gave my first public speech in the Spring of 1969 in Hogan Ballroom against the Vietnam War and ROTC. Ray and others in RSU organized the event. I tried to memorize my speech and eventually said something that sounded half way coherent. The audience gave polite applause; I think that they knew more of the war in Vietnam than I did and the applause was for the brevity of what I had to say.

A peace sign was painted on what was then the Air Force ROTC building. It is still on the roof today, a reminder of the days of intense opposition to the Vietnam War. It was never clear who painted it. Everyone I asked said that they did not know, but its painting was a victory. I suppose a symbolic victory was welcomed when we could not stop the death of millions of people in Southeast Asia. Recently I read that the College allows the symbol to stay as a symbol of debate and discussion.

There was a fire at the ROTC building where the peace sign was painted. On the night of the fire in 1970 there was a large campus wide meeting in Hogan regarding the bombing of Cambodia. An ROTC instructor, Captain Sage, said he could not comment on the Vietnam War as it was not allowed by the Marines. He said that some people could misinterpret his comments as criticism of the President. Several students yelled back that his lack of comment was a pretext and questioned his purpose for being at the meeting. SDS (mostly off campus kids) in which I was involved wanted to lead a break away demonstration from Hogan Ball Room to the ROTC building. However we could not get enough people to go and some professors whom I called misleaders argued against it. At that time anyone who argued against us was a misleaders. We lost that debate and continued to argue our points at the meeting.

Losing the debate was actually fortuitous for us as later in the meeting a voice near the door way yelled out "The ROTC building is on fire". If the fire was set, the person did it at a time that the entire left wing community at Holy Cross was at a large public meeting.

There was another fire in the same ROTC building in the Fall of 1972, but I lived off campus then and the radicals from the Class of 1972 had graduated. The adjustment to the first class of women students replaced the Vietnam War as the major issue of discussion.

The most memorable event against ROTC for me was a night demonstration in front of the ROTC building next to Loyola where the Jesuits lived. About two hundred students met there around 8 PM in the Fall of 1970 and it was dark. We started to chant "ROTC off campus" After a while the Jesuits started to hurl insults at the crowd. I supposed they were angry at us for disturbing them after dark. I was surprised as I thought the Jesuits were more long suffering.

Soon we in the demonstration started to chant "Jesuits off campus. "Of course the next day we got a bunch of criticism for our actions from many sources. Much of the criticism was for showing disrespect to the Jesuits. Eventually I saw the criticism as justified. The Jesuits are one of the more progressive Orders in the Catholic Church and an education at a Jesuit College is something immeasurably valuable. Nonetheless for me our chanting "Jesuits Off Campus" was another wonderful liberating event.

There was a cadet in the Air Force ROTC with whom I would often talk. He seemed genuinely interested in the peace movement and his personal responsibility for being an armed participant in the aggressor side of an unjust war. He later transferred to another college. He wrote and said that he did not rejoin ROTC at his new college. I had mixed feelings about his letter. I was happy that he had decided not to participate in the aggressor side of an unjust war, but I was a little troubled that I had such influence on a peer.

ROTC is still at Holy Cross today. There is still some opposition to it. An annual demonstration of Alums and students is organized by Scott, an alum. I have not gone to them on a regular basis. Although I feel the Catholic guilt for not doing so.

Today there is JROTC in the Worcester public schools. It is a clear violation of the United Nation protocols on Children Soldiers. I find the issue of ROTC at Holy Cross to be less compelling in light of the JROTC influence on Worcester's children who are increasingly poor, working class, and minority.

Chapter 9
Fat Lady

Following the lead of the Black Panthers' Free Breakfast for Children Program, activists in Worcester initiated a similar breakfast program. There were two centers for breakfast. One in Main South, run by Anne Marie. The second center was run by my roommate, Ed who eventually won a Pulitzer Prize. Ed's program was in the basement of Our Lady of Fatima Church. We called it Fat Lady, as did the children. The Church is closed today and it is likely to be demolished.

There have been some claims that Clarence ran the Free Breakfast for Children Program. I have no certain recollection of ever seeing Clarence at Fat Lady.

Every school morning for two semesters Ed organize a car load of students to get up between 5:30 and 6:00 AM and go to Fat Lady. We were mostly from the BSU, RSU, and other progressive groups. I remember Mark, Bob, and John were regulars. Although not on a regular basis, scores of other students would help out. Ed's net of recruitment went out fairly widely and it was sometimes a surprise who would show up on any given day.

Fat Lady is three or four miles from Holy Cross and we took whatever transportation Ed could organize. Many times we drove the BSU van. Once in January I had to ride in the bed of Bob's pickup truck. I learned a lot about wind chill during the ride.

Another time when Ed complained that Holy Cross did not help enough with the program. We went to see Father Brooks, who recently became President of the College and demanded that he help. Father Brooks called to Kimball dining hall and told the staff to give us surplus fry pans. What amazes me even to this day is not that Father Brooks gave us fry pans, but that he knew Kimball had surplus fry pans.

There was a time when the Pastor of Fat Lady tried to throw us out of Fat Lady. The locks were changed on the doors. At that time I saw a whole different side of Ed. He was determined to have the program reopened. He went to talk to the Pastor and we were opened for breakfast the next day.

Among the children I remember one little girl. I don't recall her name, but she used to give Ed a lot of grief. She complained about the food. She always wore red boots and she was very protective of her little brother. One time to get them to finish their food Ed told them that I would sing and dance. I waited for them to finish and then I said I had changed my mind. For some reason I could only remember "Drugstore Loving" and I thought that would not be an age appropriate song.

I talked to Ed recently. He remembers an older boy whom he felt was something of a trouble maker. Ed asked the kid to help him with the program, cleaning up and closing up. The kid's attitude changed for the better.

In the Spring we got the word that the Public Schools would be serving breakfast before classes. This made our program redundant and it was discontinued in the Fall.

When Ed returned to Holy Cross in 2005 we happened to go by Fat Lady and I could tell from his voice that he had fond memories of it, the kids, and all involved in the program.

Chapter 10
Three Black Men on Route 9

The bombings in Cambodia and the subsequent murders of four students at Kent State University in 1971 precipitated a national student strike. The student government authorized the strike and we just refused to go to class. Most students of the College joined the strike which presented a dilemma to the College administration. How could the instructors grade the students who struck?

As I recall, it was agreed that there would be no final exams and that the grade would be based on the work and tests that were already performed. Additional work could be considered by the instructors for the final grade. I did not do any additional work and left it to the Instructors to grade me as they saw fit. I can't say I got great grades, but I didn't fail any course. I took the action without regards for the consequences; a trait that those who speak truth to power seems to need once in a while.

The nationwide strike was revolutionary when judged by the standards of the IWW (Wobblies) who were most influential in the early Twentieth Century. They theorized that revolutionary social change would come about as the result of a spontaneous national strike of workers. Although we were not workers, the strike showed the strengths and the weaknesses of the student movement. On the one hand the strike had some influence on politicians and gave encouragement to the people in struggle. The strike was liberating and historic. It made many of us more confident in the struggle for political change and social justice. It showed us some of the limits of our tactics and compelled me to seek alternatives to Anarchism.

***

During the strike a demonstration was being organized in Boston, protesting the so-called Nixon incursion into Cambodia and Laos. Working with the RSU we spread the word about the demonstration. I rode into Boston with Ray and two others from the RSU.

I saw a reckless side of Ray that day. As we were travelling down the Mass Pike, Ray decided to run the tolls. As we sped through the toll lane, I could hear the toll taker yelling at us. I thought we were home free until a State Police car pulled in behind us. He seemed to have come out of nowhere. Ray was driving and said to us "Does anyone have their driver license?". I gave him my license as it did not have a photo. The trooper asked Ray to step out of the car and sit in the cruiser. Then the Trooper walked back to our car and said "Who is Gordon T. Davis?" I raised my hand.

The trooper gave me back my license and said "I could arrest you too" He then asked "He stole your license?". I didn't respond to the question. I did ask how did he knew that it was not Ray's license. The trooper said "he did not know where he lived." Ray spent the night in jail and we drove to Boston Common where the demonstration was assembling.

Every large demonstration was something of a carnival. There were people selling all sorts of left wing literature, and buttons, as well as gathering petitions. It is not much different today with the possible exception of people smoking dope. The cops stayed on the fringes and ignored the dope.

Most demonstrations have speakers who preach to the converted and to the press. They are usually boring. We were waiting for the speaker who would tell us about the alternative actions. I was laying on the grass when we heard the call to meet at a corner of the Common to march to a "secret" location to continue the protests.

We marched to Cambridge. As we marched a contingent of Boston riot cops followed. Crossing the Longfellow Bridge into Cambridge we notice that the Boston cops did not turn around and we knew then that this might be a more serious event than we anticipated. We arrived at Harvard Yard just as it was getting dark and all hell seemed to break out. It was never clear how it started, but we were in the middle of it.

A wave of cops rushed at us swinging their batons. You could not fight them as they had on their riot gear. I ran down to the Red Line and got rid of everything that could identify me as a protester, button, newspapers, and hardhat. I kept and wetted my kerchief, as I had learned during a Washington D.C. demonstration. It would be needed in case of tear gas.

When I emerged from the station I found that several of us were cut off from the main group and police had formed a line about one hundred feet from the subway entrance. I assumed they were isolating us, forcing us out of the Yard. The cops and we stood facing each other for a while and then a protester threw a brick one hundred feet into the police line. I was amazed that he could reach the line. I was more amazed that with all of their armor and shields the brick landed on the knee of an officer and he went down and then he was helped to the rear. Not much later the police realized that their position was too exposed and they moved up the street in a phalanx. We retreated. Moving back I noticed that there were tunnels in our rear and I did not want to be caught in a tunnel not knowing what was on the other side. So the cops got their way and forced the group of us out of Harvard Yard. I had enough at that point and began looking for a way back to Worcester.

The next morning I saw Al and asked what happened to him at the demonstration. He said that Jeff, Ed and he were separated from their ride and had to walk from Cambridge to Worcester. He said that they tried to hitch hike, but no one would pick up three Black men at night on Route 9. Ed, Jeff, and Al were somewhere on Main St. in Worcester when someone finally picked them up. According to Ed the driver was smoking dope and Al and Jeff joined him. Ed said he never smoked dope.

***

Whenever I bring up the story of the rebellion in Harvard Yard, my wife, Gwen, tells how she was also there. She had gone to a concert in Cambridge that evening with her friends from Fitchburg State when the rebellion took place. She tells of how she also was forced into a subway entrance. I suppose we could had been there at the same time. She says half- kiddingly that it was cosmic forces compelling us to our destiny. Sometimes I half believe her.

Chapter 11
The Black Muslims

Dean came to Holy Cross in my sophomore year. He was a Black Muslim and he changed the dynamics of the Black Student Union. Dean had a value system to support his opinions and the discussions among the Black students became more serious and pointed. Any discussion after Dean's arrival at the BSU meeting could take a turn to who was really Black and who was a friend of "the devil" (White people).

The Black students respected, but disagreed with Dean and the three other students who later joined the Black Muslim, Carlton, Harmon, and Doug. Doug has changed his name to an Islamic one and is today a great supporter of the College. Although I think Doug is not held in the same esteem as other Black Alums with non Muslim names by the White Alumni and Administration. Perhaps this will change with the election of Barrack Obama.

Dean had a black belt in Karate and he would hold lessons in Hogan. Almost all of the Black students signed up. Many White students resented this. Some complained to the administration and once the student manager of Hogan tried to stop a Karate lesson by asking Dean for a license to teach Karate. The manager left after no one responded to his request and he did not return.

There was no Temple in Worcester but there was an Imam, Mr. Shabazz, who held services in various locations. His daughter, Lambmie, married Elijah, a roommate of Ed and me. Elijah never went to the Temple, while I went a few times.

One time Dean convinced me to go to the Temple in Roxbury. I did not know what to expect, but I was curious. Upon arriving I noticed that there were body guards called the Fruit of Islam standing between the pulpit and the attendees. Other than that it was not much different in format than Protestant churches I attended. I think Don Muhammad was the Imam. At the end of the service the Imam asked everyone new to the Temple to stand. About six of us stood up. He then asked us to join the Temple. Two people agreed. Everyone was looking at us who did not want to join. Embarrassed I sat back down.

While driving back to campus I became very hungry. We had not eaten since early morning and there was no food after the service at the Temple. When we got back to campus Kimball dining hall was closed. So I had to spend some of the very little money I had on dinner at Hogan. I ordered a hamburger with french fries. Dean, standing next to me, starting to eat some of my fries without asking. My hunger caused me to snap at him. I told him not to touch anything on my tray. If I had enough discipline not to eat until I got to the table, he should have had enough discipline to ask me to share my food. Instead of apologizing, Dean said if I had no french fries I would survive. It is funny that I still hold a grudge about the french fries and his rebuke.

I thought that the Black Muslim were fundamentally wrong in their analysis of how to achieve social justice. It could not be achieved by isolating ourselves from other working people of other races. Now I believe there is no race among people; everyone is Black. White people are Black people who don't accept that they are Black. At the time I thought that Malcolm X had a better analysis for the struggle for social and economic justice.

What absolutely convinced me that the Black Muslims were a dead end was their crazy belief that there was a spaceship in orbit about the Earth, manned by Japanese, who were going to bring justice to the White race in the form of a nuclear apocalypse.

When I moved off campus I had less and less contact with the Black Muslims. I last remember Dean driving through a march against ROTC and one of the students banged his car with his hand. Dean was angry and I spoke with him to calm him down. I looked at him differently after that because he had a car (I thought only the rich kids had cars) and drove through a protest march. Dean like myself eventually left Holy Cross without graduating. I suppose he too felt some alienation at the College

Chapter 12
Getting Over

During senior year Ed, Elijah, and I were roommates in what was the RA suite on the Black corridor. The room was intended for three roomies. When Ed's previous roommates left. he asked that we join him. If Elijah and I had not, Ed might have been forced to live in a room that was not a suite. It worked out fine as Elijah's family was in Worcester and he spent a lot of time with them. I also had a shared apartment in Worcester on Piedmont St. I shared the apartment with Mark, class of '72, and his girlfriend, Patti.

The summer before senior year in 1971 Mark and Patti went to their respective homes in Connecticut. So John and I needed additional roommates to share the expenses. Gil was looking for a place to stay over the summer and he joined us as did Al. The living conditions became a little tight and John eventually moved out.

In preparation for the summer we took cereal and can fruit from Kimball. All the students would take food and bring it to their dorm rooms where they would eat it between dining hours. We did it to eat over the summer. Gil used to call it "getting over" Needless to say the food only lasted a month.

Gil got a job at a tire place, where he rethreaded tires. I worked at Head Start as a teacher's aide. A job that Lenny, a Holy Cross transfer student. got for me. The lead teacher was

Mrs. Foley, the mother of Jack "the shot" Foley. Jack Foley was a star of Holy Cross basketball before I came to the College. Mrs. Foley was a great teacher and manager. I enjoyed working in her class. I enjoyed the field trips as much as the students did. Subsequently she became a member of the Worcester School Committee.

During the summer Harvey came to our apartment. I still don't know how he found us. With him was a girl from Seattle, Becky. From the way she talked I assumed that she was a runaway. Harvey and Becky stayed a few days, but they had to leave as Gil complained about them using up our resources. I had to agree with Gil as he paid his share of rent and Harvey and Becky did not. That was the last time I saw Harvey. I heard he overdosed somewhere in the Mid West. I don't know what happened to Becky.

Harvey was a guy I could never figure out. When in high school he was full of hubris and although we hung out together I cannot say we were good friends. During the first semester of his freshman year at Holy Cross Harvey had a son and married his son's mother. I only met her once or twice. Harvey was banned from living in the dorms as the College policy was that married students had to live off campus. Harvey lasted only through the Spring of 1969 and then he dropped out.

Before leaving the apartment with Becky, Harvey and I discussed politics. He thought I was naïve and somewhat limited in knowledge. He said that I should travel more, especially to mountain states and the South where some people were hostile to left wing ideas. He said I would lose my optimism. I still find it hard to accept his death.

Al was my good buddy, but at times during that summer he would annoy me. He did not work and he would bum money off me all the time. At times it was OK, such as when we would buy cheap beer or wine and share the bottle. Eventually he started to buy ale as he said that the cheap beer gave him nightmares. Other times he upset me, such as when I came home from work and Al was playing the record player so loudly that it could be heard down the street. I asked him to turn it down as I did not want to annoy the neighbors. Al had a son with the daughter of a minister in Worcester, but I lost contact with them.

That summer was a turning point for me and my summer roommates. We had broken the ties to our respective parents' homes. I still feel a bit of sadness when thinking of that summer as I would never quite feel that my home in Philadelphia was the only place that could be home. Subsequently I would never spend more than a week at my parent's home during any one visit. My concept of home had changed and expanded.

Chapter 13
Black Coalition

In 1970 several cases of police brutality occurred in Worcester. In August the Black people of Worcester met at the Kitty Kat Lounge on North Main St. owned by Betty Price, a community leader. At the meeting a list of grievances were drawn up and the people started to march down Main St. to present their grievances to City Council. On the way several windows were broken and the police arrested several of the marchers. It was my understanding that the City Council ran and hid that night.

It would not be the last time that the City Council had to end a meeting due to the anger of the people regarding police brutality. In 1993 people from the community gathered at Centro Las Americas, a community center, and then marched on City Council over the homicide of Christino Hernandez, a Hispanic Man, by the Worcester Police.

When I returned to campus in September 1970 I learned about the Black Coalition. The consensus leaders of the organization were Lenny, a resident of Worcester and a Holy Cross student, Bobby, a resident of Worcester, and Betty. The Black Coalition was open to just about everyone and I joined.

For the Fall we had joined up with the RSU at Holy Cross to raise money for the Defense Fund for those who were arrested in August. We decided to put on a concert at Fitton Field. After all was said and done the RSU lost money. I learned a lesson that sometimes it is best to just ask for donations than to put on an event.

Lenny was the real driving force behind the Black Coalition. Later my good friend Elijah, a resident of Worcester and student at Holy Cross, and my best buddy at the time, Al, would join. We met every two weeks and to some extent we changed the character of the Black Coalition to something similar to the Black Panthers. We were legally armed, we ran social programs, and put out a left leaning newspaper. At this point Greg, a resident of Worcester, helped us with arms safety.

A large part of what we did could be considered the civil rights movement in the urban North, but it is mostly forgotten as were the hundreds of thousand actions by other activists. Lenny had us become involved in a boycott of Thom McCann Shoes when it treated Black workers in a disparate manner. At that time there was a large distributor on Millbrook St. and a retail store on Main St. We choose to picket the Main St. store as there was a side walk and it had visibility. We picketed for a week or so until Thom McCann made some concessions. I did not like picketing that much; there were several White people who would say racist things to us. I thought that they were mentally ill and ignored them, but Lenny would once in a while engage them. I see those same White people in the contemporaneous Tea Party.

During the early seventies the CEO of a large insurance company in Worcester wanted to tear down the Black neighborhood of Laurel-Clayton and put up a project named after himself, Plumley Village. His insurance company, State Mutual, began to buy up the houses with promissory notes; people gave up title without getting payment. Months went by and there were no payments. In response Lenny organized the people from the Laurel- Clayton neighborhood to march up to the new State Mutual building on Lincoln St. Students from the colleges especially Holy Cross and Clark University joined the march. The demonstration was stronger with the multi- racial unity. Some demonstrators sat down on the lawn of the insurance company and waited to be arrested; one of them was Anne Marie who would run the Breakfast Program in Main South. I did not join them as I did not at the time see the logic of getting arrested to make a point.

The brutality by the Worcester Police continued through the Winter and we made a decision to have a rally at City Hall. We marched from the two neighborhoods in which there were relatively large Black populations, Laurel-Clayton and Main South. Bobby led the march from Laurel Clayton and Lenny led the march from Main South. We bought walkie-talkies to coordinate the march. Greg suggested a radio wave length and it was coincidently the same as the Worcester Police. We all had a laugh as we listened to the cops scramble to a new channel.

In the Spring of 1971 the BSU collaborated on a protest of the Attica Massacre of prisoners by authorities and the murder of George Jackson, a Black Panther. Many but not all of the BSU came to the protest at the Worcester County Jail. The protesters were half Worcester residents and half BSU members. In keeping with the Black Panther principle of protecting our own we had marshals armed with batons. I still can see Darryl looking strong with his baton and hard hat ready to do battle.

In order to have the demonstration on Summer St. we needed a permit. We had a heated argument in the group whether we should even acknowledge the power of the state and get the permit. The consensus was that there was no need for senseless arrests. I was assigned the task of getting the permit from the Worcester Police. Once again I had to go into the police station. Everything went OK until the Lieutenant began to question me about why we wanted to protest. I told him that it was about the massacre at Attica. I wanted to leave and not get into a debate with him. As I stood to leave he loudly said "You just want to cause trouble!" I did not say anything back and left. Although I have been called a trouble maker before and after, it was not the right time to have a debate with the cops. We would make our points in the streets.

At our next meeting we discussed the implication of the incident and Lenny said that the detective was just annoyed and that it probably meant nothing. So we went ahead with plans. Fortunately the police stayed away and there were no incidents. This may have been the first armed protest in Worcester since the rebellions against slavery.

What many considered the high point of the Black Coalition was our cooperation with the City Health Dept. in the Sickle Cell Anemia test program. We covered about half of the Black population in the City. It worked so well that a foundation offered ten-thousand dollars in grant money for the next cooperative project with the City. Unfortunately no one seemed to have time or expertise to write a grant. I made an attempt, but it was inadequate.

One of the issues that arose in the Sickle Anemia program was that some people did not want to be tested as they did not know how the information would be used. Others people said that they preferred not to know. These are the same issue that people face with the present day genetic testing. Unlike today there were no laws protecting people from the misuse of medical diagnosis in the 1970's,

There were many people in the Black Coalition, but nothing lasts forever. Al avoided the draft only to be stopped for a traffic violation and he was forced to join the army. Greg felt that we could not continue to maintain our level of organizing and he quit. Lenny continued to work, but he too devoted less time to the organization. Bobby left town. Betty became the Executive Director of Prospect House which had its roots with the organizing of Abbie Hoffmann.

By the Winter of 1972/73 the Black Coalition was no longer effectively functioning.

***

At the time my concept of the police was pretty negative. I saw the brutality of the cops. I was unjustly arrested four times and all of the charges were eventually dismissed. However my view of the police has evolved with experience. My first arrest was by officer Reardon who stopped me while walking to my apartment on Piedmont Street in 1971 (walking while Black). He asked me what I was doing. I said that I was walking home. He asked what was my name I told him my name (I was not legally required to do so at that time). He demanded ID. I said I had no ID. At that point he arrested me for disorderly conduct. Today my son and other Black young men face the same issues. I was appointed a public defender who never appeared at my trial. The judge dismissed the case.

Another arrest was during the integration of Boston Schools in 1975. After some racists throw rocks at the school children going to South Boston High a group of us wanted to greet the children and to protest the racism. While on the bus in Dorchester and with a permit for the event at South Boston the police arrested eighty (80) of us, charging us with inciting to riot. Of course this charge was dismissed.

My last arrest was during a demonstration in which a "Grand Wizard "of the KKK came to Boston. I was standing near a group of cops when for no apparent reason one of them grabbed me. When taken to lock up the police throw me to floor and used a choker until I nearly passed out. I was charged with "yelling". As before the charges were dismissed.

During the Sickle Anemia campaign Lenny, Elijah, and I were nearly arrested when the Worcester Tactical Squad had nothing better to do than hang out in Main South neighborhood harassing people. We were leaving a site for the Sickle Cell Anemia testing, "Your Place". It was located near Gilreins on Main St. As we were leaving we jogged to our car a few blocks up the street as we were late for another event. Driving away toward

Cambridge St. Elijah said, "don't stare, but the cars in front and back of us are unmarked police cars". We drove like this trying figure out what was going on until we reached Cambridge St. which had a left turn lane. I put on my turn signal to turn left and the lead police car went into the left lane. Then Elijah said to go straight and don't turn. We passed the lead car and the police car behind us stopped following as their tactical exercise was ruined. We turned left at Stafford St. and pulled into the back of Big Boy restaurant in case the cops came looking for us. We were late for the meeting, but we had a good laugh at our good fortune.

During the 1980's I started to coach youth soccer and there were a lot of police parents. I am especially grateful to Mrs. Rich who so much helped my son with his reading and Lt. Trotta who coached my son. I got to know them as people. I came to accept that some cops are not intentionally brutal and some are. Like at South Boston High School all of the police follow orders no matter how bogus.

Chapter 14
Progressive Labor Party

Students for a Democratic Society (SDS) split into at least three separate organizations in 1970 and 1971. The largest faction was the Worker Student Alliance led by the Progressive Labor Party (PLP). The other factions were the Weathermen and a Trotsky-like group which later became associated with the Chinese Communist Party. The Weathermen were anarchists who used terrorist methods. I am still amazed how some young people today apologize for the Weather underground; they will say that I needed to have experienced the Sixties to understand the Weathermen. The irony is I did experience the Sixties and reject the Weather men individualist terrorist tactics.

In Worcester there were SDS people who sided with PLP against the Weathermen. I met them at an anti war rally at Holy Cross. Neil and I hit it off almost immediately. There was an energy and charisma about him. Unfortunately he lacked self disciple. When he went to California, he and a friend were convicted of armed robbery of a gas station.

I recalled that after a rally Neil shouted out that there would be a get together at his apartment. To our surprise one of the right wing kids went. At the party a joint came around. I did not want to seem ungrateful, so like Clinton I did not inhale. I never smoked cigarettes and smoking was physically tough for me. The right wing kid passed on the joint and I suspect he wanted to leave. He had to wait for the rest of us as we stayed a few hours more. We saw less of him after that.

In 1971 I met Bob and his wife Cathy who were the organizers in Worcester for PLP. Bob and Cathy tried their best to recruit people to PLP, but they were mostly unsuccessful. They moved to Boston as collectively agreed in their club. Their disciplined action in moving to Boston was very impressive as it showed that the members of PLP were serious about their goals, unlike other self described revolutionaries.

This discipline of PLP made a lot of people angry as PLP would vote as a bloc at the SDS meetings and speak of revolution in a manner that exposed many as just arm chair revolutionaries or worse. PLP thought the Communist Party USA was just the left wing of the Democratic Party. PLP hated the Weathermen as government inspired anarcho-terrorists who mainly scared off the working class.

In 1971 PLP held its first May Day demonstration. I felt guilty about not going. When I went in 1972; it was exhilarating, marching under red flags and calling for the end of capitalism. I still go to May Day marches. I sang at the May Day dinner in 2009. My wife says that my singing was bad but my ideas were good.

In the Spring of 1972 was the PLP led SDS convention at Harvard University. Henry was the BSU president then and he wanted to go. Eventually six members of the BSU went. We stayed at Bob's house and slept in his living room. Henry wanted to go to make contact with people from around the country as did some of the others. Some of us went to learn more. It was a tough convention, as the moderator lost control of it and confusion erupted. Eventually someone got us back on track and there was a good flow of ideas.

What PLP advocated was intriguing. In 1964 it said that the Soviet Union was a state capitalist country. In 1971 it said that China was also a state capitalist country when the working class, led by Red Guards, was defeated by revisionist forces led by Mao. In 1974 it said Cuba was not a communist country and was on the road back to capitalism, in spite of its armies defeating the racist South Africans in Angola.

In the USA PLP said the War in Vietnam was not a mistake by Kennedy and Johnson, it was an intentional form of Imperialism meant to control oil reserves in the South China Seas.

Most importantly they said that racism hurt everyone and that the only way racism would be defeated was through multi racial unity and an end to capitalism. Nationalist groups such as Ron Karenga, the Panthers, and the Black Muslims were dead ends.

I eventually joined PLP and the political work became more important than school work. To a certain extent the line of PLP has proven true in regards to the regression of the Soviet Union, China, and Cuba back to capitalism. PLP predicted these event twenty years before they became obvious. We are still studying the events from the vantages of Marxist theory. The forces behind the regression is very little studied by the traditional historians or economists. It is a burning question for us who hold tightly to the values of to each according to need and from each according to ability.

Chapter 15
The Prettiest Girl in Fitchburg

During the summer of 1972 I again worked at Head Start. This second time at Head Start was not as interesting as the first. Mrs. Foley was no longer there and the chemistry was different. The field trips were the same and did not have novelty. I enjoyed working with the children in the Cambridge St. / Canterbury St area. It is easy to see why so many students chose to be teachers.

Also during the Summer of 1972 I taught literacy in the Worcester County Jail on Summer St. Henry who was the BSU president was going home to Philadelphia for the Summer and he asked me if I would take over the class until he returned. Reluctantly I said OK. I hate being locked up and I felt uncomfortable with police or in this case corrections officers.

During the 1970s and today many of the prisoners are Black or Hispanic. Everyone I taught in jail was a so called minority. Each time I went to class in jail I felt an enormous sadness and depression. It took me all night to shake off the funk.

The books I chose for reading were left wing books and eventually the Sheriff kicked me out. I did not return to the Worcester County Jail until recently when I went on a fact finding visit with the ACLU.

***

Mark and Patti graduated in 1972 and the apartment on Piedmont St was no longer available to me. Ray, a former Holy Student and some friends had an apartment on Castle St. and they asked me to take over the rent. The apartment was relatively cheap at fifty five dollars a month. The neighborhood was in Main South which some people considered to be a rough area; but it was to me a relatively nice place compared to North Philly.

When the gas bill for the apartment came I noticed that there was a balance that Ray had not paid. So I told the gas company that I was a new tenant. The gas company turned off the gas. Their policy was that new tenants were considered new customers and that I had to make a deposit of two hundred dollars. I could not come up with the deposit so I went without heat and hot water. When the pipes burst in December of 1972 I had to move out. For a few weeks I was homeless and stayed with friends.

***

In January 1973 I subletted a room from Jay, a Holy Cross student in the Class of 1974. Peter, also in the Class of 1974, subletted another room from Jay. Jay eventually became a criminal defense attorney in the Boston area and I feel nostalgic whenever he appears on television. I recently saw him on the Emily Rooney show talking about the shooter in the Giffords case.

I remember when he and I went to an anti-death penalty hearing near the turn of this century. When I approach him he didn't recognize me as I had a full beard and long hair. My wife says at the time I looked like a homeless person. Jay must have thought so as well, before I identified myself.

Peter after graduation worked for a social justice group and he helped to expose the slave like conditions of immigrants in North Carolina' poultry industry.

Jay subletted a fourth bed room to Mike, a student at Worcester State College. Mike was then and is now very religious. He eventually became a professor at area colleges and my son took some of his courses.

***

I flunked out of Holy Cross for the second time in December of 1972. I think back on my flunking out of Holy Cross and the explanation that makes the most sense to me is what I call the Bob Dylan syndrome. Robert Zimmerman had enrolled at the University of Minnesota and never attended class. There was so much creativity going on outside of the classroom that he was overwhelmed by it. For me the excitement of the events and potential of 1972 was intoxicating.

***

In January 1973 I started work at US Steel as a machine operator, I made oil well cables. It was the first job I applied for after the Christmas of 1972. It was a union job and it paid relatively well with benefits. I lucked out as 1973 and 1974 turned out to be tough years for the national economy with high unemployment and disruptive oil embargo. While at US Steel I began to organize with the goal of moving my union brothers and sisters to the left. I learned as much from them as they learned from me. I still see some of them once in a while and we talk of our fight against the bosses. Sadly one of my union brothers, Harry, just died in 2011.

***

In 1973 the Yum Kippur War caused an oil embargo by OPEC. There were no gas stations open on Sundays during the gasoline shortage and sometimes you could only buy gas on particular days based on your license plate.

My dad came to visit after I started to work at U.S. Steel and I asked that he look for a car for me as I could now make payments. Within a few weeks he came back with a Volkswagen Fastback. It was a car that gave me constant trouble, but I got over one hundred and fifty thousand miles out of it before I gave it away to my brother who had moved to the Worcester area. The Fastback proved to be a useful car during the oil embargo. It was able to go to Philadelphia and back on one tank of gas plus a five gallon gas can. My brother and I had our best discussions during those rides to Philly and I always looked forward to them.

***

At an event in Worcester I met Tom, an insurance salesman. He invited me over to his house and I met his wife, Lydia. My first impression of her was that she was smart and sophisticated. At some point in the Spring of 1973 Lydia said that her sister Gwen wanted to go with us to the old El Morocco Restaurant then located in a three decker building on the East Side of Worcester.

Even though I was with my friend, Susan, I could not take my eyes off of Gwen. She was gorgeous and I still say that I married the prettiest girl in Fitchburg. On our first date Gwen and I went to Paul's Mall, a now defunct night club, in Boston. Jerry Butler was performing. Although we were both Catholic, we argued about abortion all the way into Boston. We stopped arguing while at the club, but it did not seem likely that there would be a second date. About two weeks later Tom called me and said that Gwen wanted me to call her. When I called she said yes to another date. Many years later we found out that Lydia and Tom conspired to make sure that Gwen and I would go on a second date. Tom just made up the story that Gwen had spoken to him about wanting me to call her. Lydia had told Gwen a similar story of how I wanted a second date. I guess there were cosmic forces at work to bring Gwen and me together. We have been married now for over thirty six years.

In 1973 I made interesting new friends and I met my wife. I also got my first car and I got a reasonably good job during a recession and I continued to organize albeit in a new location. My going to Holy Cross almost completely changed who I was to someone else almost unrecognizable even to myself. That trip to heaven had ended and I felt my real life was about to be different, a life after heaven.

CPSIA information can be obtained at www.ICGtesting.com
Printed in the USA
LVOW11s2356041113

359957LV00020B/798/P